ART JOURNAL

For Girls

CW00730967

Savvy Stationery

Published by Amazon on behalf of Savvy Stationery. No part of this book may be reproduced or transmitted in any form or by any means, electronic or mechanical, including photocop or by any information storage, without written permission from the publisher. All right remain with original artists of the below mentioned elements.

Design attribution: Book cover - Beaandbloom.com, kavalenkavadesign, Sketchify Philippines, Jemastock2, Allies Interactive, Sparklestroke, Rudchenko

Wildlife in the Wildflowers

Draw insects, bugs and any wildlife you would expect to find in your garden or local park.

Draw the Food

DONUT

ICE-CREAM

SANDWICH

Feather Patterns

Create you own decorative feather with a mixture of lines, circles and random shapes. Try to be as detailed as possible!

Flower Art Study

Pick a flower or find a vase of flowers to draw. Look at all the details on each flower head before you start drawing. Add colour to your artwork.

Abstract Art

Abstract art is art that is made up of different shapes, lines and colours; like in the examples below. It can be really fun to do and even more fun to try and decide what the drawing is about. What do you think the art below means? Could the art on the left be about space? Create your own abstract art in the empty boxes below!

Draw your favourite animal at the zoo

Design your own
T-shirt with something
you love

My Self Portrait

All great artists draw self portraits! Sit in front of a mirror and draw your face in the frame above. Make sure to include your name and age.

Draw a picture of your pet, or a pet you wish you had

Draw an Underwater Scene

Draw a monster with three eyes

Draw an ice cream cone

Draw a house or where you live

Mandala Colouring

Landscape Art

Instructions: Start by choosing a colour for your background. It can be any colour depending on your mood. Colour in the background smoothly. Using a black pen draw a forest full of trees over your colourful background.

Materials
- Colouring pencils
- Black pen
- Your imagination!

Draw the Animal

DOLPHIN

MOUSE

OWL

Dot Art Drawing

Drawing with only dots is a form of art called Pointillism. Using tiny dots a drawing can look like a painted picture from far away. Using only dots fill in the flower below.

Then try to create your own flower in the space provided using only dots.

Learn to shade

Shading gives a more real appearance to your drawings. Shade is the darkest part of an object. Below are examples of how you can add shade/shadow to your drawings - using hatching (left) and stippling (right). Give these techniques a go on the empty circles for a 3D effect.

Object Study

Collect two objects from around your home and place them on a table in front of you. Study the object and shadows as you draw them.

Create a Colouring Page

Draw a scene (ideas: beach, mountains or playground) in the box below. Use colouring pencils fill in the colouring key with the colours you want your scene to be coloured in with, making sure to label each colour.

Then pass this page to a family member or friend to colour in your very own colouring page!

COLOURING
KEY:

○ White   ○   ○   ○

○   ○   ○

Mandala Art

A mandala is a geometric design or pattern that is created using symmetry. Create your own mandala below.

Butterflies

Floral

Draw a bird sat on its nest

Draw a mouse nibbling a piece of cheese

Draw a friendly looking spider

Draw a starry nights sky with a full moon

Draw a rainbow

Line Art

Keeping your pencil on the page at all times, attempt to draw these three line art drawings below.

3D Shapes

Match the shapes to their correct name:

  Cone

  Sphere

  Cube

  Cylinder

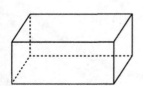 Rectangular prism

Drawing from Nature

Collect dry leaves and stick in the box below. In the 2nd box draw your leaf collection.

Draw what makes you unique!

Draw the weather

RAIN

SUNSHINE

A STORM

Mountain Wildlife

Draw three amimals you would expect to find in the mountains.

Draw what you think an alien would look like

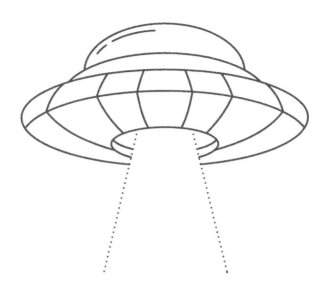

Draw exactly what you can see around you

Draw something round
and then something
square

Draw a piece of fruit and give it a face with arms and legs

Draw an object found in your bedroom

Draw someone you love very much

My Future Self

Draw an imaginary portrait of yourself as an adult. Think about what your hair will be like & how you might have changed.

My Famous Masterpiece

Print out a famous work of art from the internet and stick it in the box below.

Now draw your own version of the artwork in any style you like - have fun with it!

Pebble Art

Draw patterns and add colour to this stack of pebbles.
Make sure to add lots of detail.

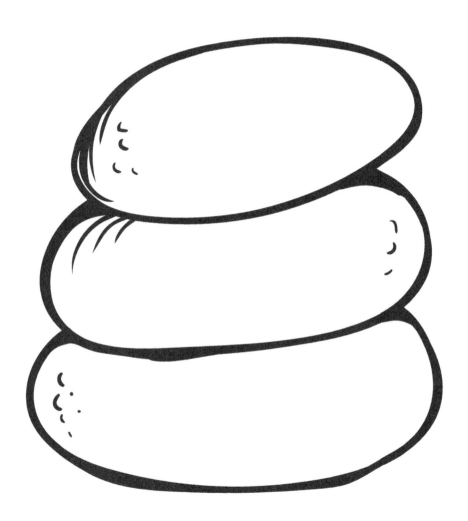

Drawing Buildings

Drawing buildings is all about angles and dimension to make your drawing appear more real - this can be really tricky to do! A person that draws and designs buildings is called an Architect.

Try to design and draw your own building, below.

Draw your family

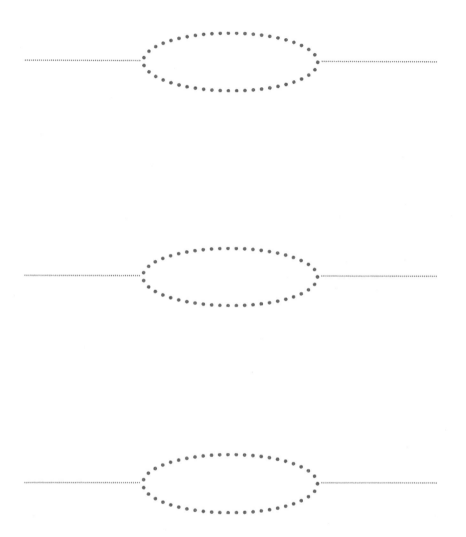

Symmetry Drawing

A drawing that is symmetric has identical parts mirroring each other across a line of symmetry. In nature both butterflies and leaves are symmetrical. Try to draw the wings of these butterflies, making sure all the lines and shapes are the same as the other wing.

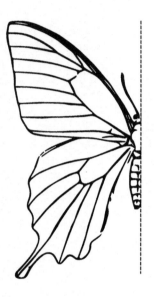

Draw an animal of your choice riding a bicycle

Mandala Colouring

Mandala Colouring

Draw a rocket travelling to a planet in space

Draw your favourite book or tv show

Draw a sunny day at the beach

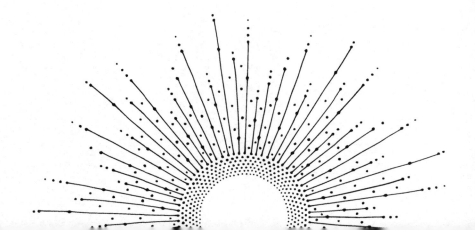

Ask a family member or friend what you should draw today

Draw an igloo

Create you own chocolate bar

Create your own bar of chocolate. Design the packaging and remember to give your chocolate bar a name!

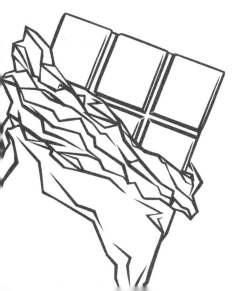

Name: _____

Typography

Typography is the name for different shapes of letters and how they look on a page - below are some examples of how the same words can look different when using different letter shapes and styles. Try writing your name in these three styles.

Silhouettes

A silhouette is the outline of a shape, person or object and is filled in black. This means there are no details other than the shape/outline. Below you can see a silhouette of a girl and a cat. Try creating your own silhouette of someone in your family or a pet.

Draw an object found in your house and give it a face

Fantasy Drawing

Draw a fantasy scene from your imagination. Here are a few ideas - underwater scene with mermaids, mythical scene including a casle and unicorn.

Fashion Designer

Be your own fashion designer and design an outfit you would enjoy wearing! Make sure to include shoes and accessories.

Draw a picnic and include all the food you enjoy eating

Draw a school of fish

Draw a wobbly jelly

Draw your favourite outfit

Draw something magical

Draw a cat wearing a hat

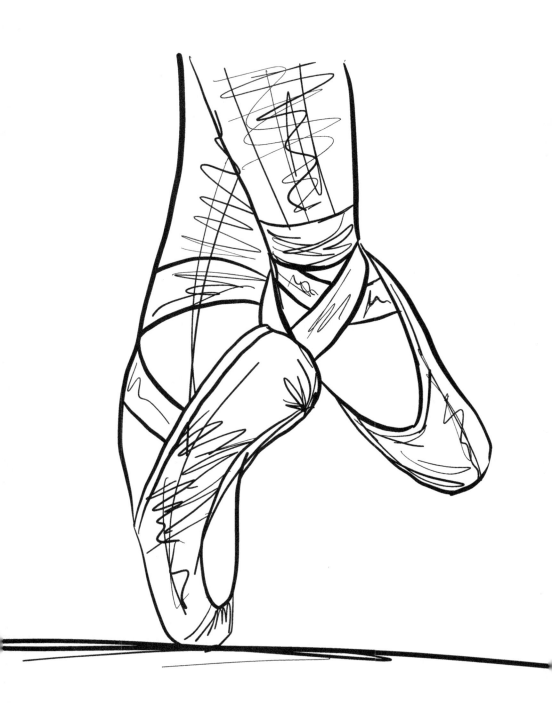

Doodle Page

Doodle Page

Doodle Page

Doodle Page

Doodle Page

Doodle Page

Doodle Page

Doodle Page

Doodle Page

Doodle Page

Doodle Page

Doodle Page

Doodle Page

Doodle Page

Doodle Page

Doodle Page

Doodle Page

Printed in Great Britain
by Amazon

53763421R00056